HOME MADE CRAFTING

AN UNOFFICIAL BEGINNERS GUIDE TO LEARN TO USE CRICUT MACHINE WITH USEFUL TIPS, TRICKS, AND EASY PROJECTS FOR STARTING!

ELEANOR NELSON

CONTENTS

Introduction	v
1. Cricut Machine: What Is It	1
2. The Cricut Maintenance: Do It Easy	31
3. Design Space: How To Set Up Your First Custom Project	37
4. Tips And Tricks On How To Create Canvas	46
5. Projects For Beginners	70
Conclusions	109

© **Copyright 2021 by Eleanor Nelson - All rights reserved**.

This document is geared towards providing exact and reliable information in regard to the topic and issue covered.

- From a Declaration of Principles which was accepted and approved equally by a Committee of the American Bar Association and a Committee of Publishers and Associations.

In no way is it legal to reproduce, duplicate, or transmit any part of this document in either electronic means or in printed format. All rights reserved.

The information provided herein is stated to be truthful and consistent, in that any liability, in terms of inattention or otherwise, by any usage or abuse of any policies, processes, or directions contained within is the solitary and utter responsibility of the recipient reader. Under no circumstances will any legal responsibility or blame be held against the publisher for any reparation, damages, or monetary loss due to the information herein, either directly or indirectly.

Respective authors own all copyrights not held by the publisher.

The information herein is offered for informational purposes solely and is universal as so. The presentation of the information is without contract or any type of guarantee assurance.

The trademarks that are used are without any consent, and the publication of the trademark is without permission or backing by the trademark owner. All trademarks and brands within this book are for clarifying purposes only and are owned by the owners themselves, not affiliated with this document.

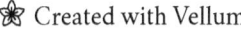 Created with Vellum

INTRODUCTION

A Cricut is a cutting system that helps you to cut and make beautiful and amazing crafts with materials that you didn't even know existed, that's the short answer. You can also sketch, emboss and produce folding lines to realize 3D designs, birthday cards, boxes, etc. depending on the layout you have.

When you have two or three projects in mind, look at your current crafting supplies. Do you have the majority of materials for one of those projects? If so, start with that one! If not, put all three projects in a hat and draw one. If you like it, do it. If you feel a pang of sadness because you drew the name of a project you really did not want, then do the one you discovered you want to do!

The Cricut machine has a number of usages in addition to being a cutter machine for a scrapbooking design. It is possible to make use of the designs to produce items like welcoming memory cards, wall surface decorations, therefore a lot more. You need to believe artistically. There are actually no borders, as well as they're all a figment of your creative imagination if there are any.

The Cricut machine is user-friendly and versatile. There is hardly a limit to what you can do with your machine, and the projects can be fun and as challenging as you want to make them.

There are plenty of decorations you can make using these machines, whether it's for Christmas, Halloween, or other seasonal-themed decorations. Perhaps you are looking for something more permanent, like unique hanging planters.

CHAPTER ONE

CRICUT MACHINE: WHAT IS IT

A CRICUT MACHINE (also known as a craft plotter or die-cutting machine) is a personal cutting machine. It is similar to a desktop printer; images and designs printed on a computer are sent to the machine. Except that instead of printing the design, the machine moves a blade around to cut out the desired material.

A Cricut machine is considered a die-cutting machine. Today, they no longer have cartridges because they do not need them anymore. Now, everything is done digitally. This lets you use any font or shape you want, as long as it is on your computer. These machines are advanced now, so they work over Bluetooth or Wi-Fi, which enables you to design straight from your iPad, iPhone, or computer, whichever is your personal preference.

The amazing thing is that, with a Cricut, you are only limited by your own creativity because there is so much out there for you to use. The Cricut is compared to a printer in some ways. When you have a printer, there is a design that you created on your computer and then you print it out. The difference is that, with a Cricut machine, you will cut the design out of whatever material you choose.

Each machine has different ways of cutting things, and you will notice this, depending on which machine you get. You can make different things with them as well. You can cut fun shapes for scrapbooking (this is considered a lost art or an older generation activity, but it is very entertaining and a great way for preserving memories) and design T-shirts, leather bracelets, stickers for your car, or envelopes. The options are endless when you are creating your own designs, and all of them are fun and can be used as business options for people as well.

This machine is great for precision cutting, for crafting, but it is important to know that, while the paper is one of the many things that it can cut, it is not the only thing. It can cut so much more which is something that we will be going into in a later chapter. They can also score material, which makes folding easy and crisp to give it a professional look, and it can write and draw with pens.

WHAT CAN THE CRICUT DO?

When you break it down to its most basic operation, the Cricut does two things. It cuts and it draws. These two functions, however, have over a million uses and can be used on hundreds of materials, making it a truly versatile crafting powerhouse. Breaking it down to these two features seems almost like an injustice to the adaptability and versatility that this machine truly has.

The Cricut Design Space library contains drawings of different colors, with which you can cut materials, or you can decide to input your own image and drawings using Photoshop, your tablet, or Illustrator. You can also draw a hand sketch, scan it into your machine to draw and cut for you materials such as paper, vinyl, craft foam, fabric, metal, faux leather, sticker paper and even adhesive sheets.

There are models of the machine that allow users to

use a pen rather than cutting to write texts and draw images and can be used to produce wedding and party invitations that look handwritten.

The designs are digitally stored, thus, users can select and edit different patterns on their personal computers or mobile devices. Furthermore, there is a Cricut Image Library with over 50,000 images, fonts and projects that users can choose from.

CRICUT MODELS: WHICH IS THE BEST FOR ME?

Have you ever wondered about the history of the circuit machine? If you don't have a clear idea of the history of the Cricut, don't be frustrated because you are about to learn about the different circuit machines that have been used to date. Cricut machines are in the first place known to be produced by the Novelty and Provo Craft.

And Provo Craft's location is in Utah; this company has been around for about 15 years; it was first created on December 21, 2003. And here are the different models of Cricut from this machine.

The Cricut Personal

The Cricut Personal/V1 machine was primarily designed for the operation of this machine with Cricut cartridges. This machine is considered a standalone machine.

The Cricut Cuttlebutt

The Cricut Cuttlebug machine is characterized by being compatible with most of the leading brands of embossed folders and stars. This machine includes a B-plate - a cutter, an A-plate - a spacer, a C-plate - and an adapter (but these parts are usually sold separately. There are different thicknesses, and this helps with matching and blending.

The Cricut BrightPad

Cricut BrightPad generally comes in Mint Green and Rose Gold. It's a modern lightbox type and works great for tracing, de-fouling, piecing, jewelry making, and paper cake.

The Cricut Gypsy

The Cricut Gypsy was primarily a portable personal design device used with the Cricut® Personal, Create, Expression, cake, cake mini, expression two, and imagine machines. Cricut Gypsy allows you to store the contents of the Cricut® cartridge, design with the contents, then connect to the Cricut machine to cut.

The joy of Cricut

This version of the Cricut machine was introduced on February 12, 2020, and became available in March 2020. The Cricut Joy is smaller; it is a lighter version at about 5" x 8"; and less than about 4 pounds. Cricut Joy generally introduces two features that are not available elsewhere in the Cricut portfolio. The Cricut Joy helps cut single designs to about 4 feet long and repeated at about 20 feet with exceptional materials and accessories.

Easy Press Cricut:

Cricut Easy Press generally comes in three different sizes and is used to heat iron-on vinyl. You may also find that it has similar uses to an iron-on.

The creator of Cricut

(Released on August 20, 2017; the Cricut Maker machine is generally used with Design Space, which is considered an online cloud-based software. This Cricut machine does not work as a standalone machine. When you want to use Design Space on top of a desktop or laptop, you generally need an internet connection. And when using the Cricut machine with the Design Space app on either an iOS iPhone or iPad device, you can use the offline feature in the app to use the machine and Design Space without an Internet connection. Cricut Maker is considered a versatile machine with interchangeable scoring and cutting heads.

A Cricut explores the Air

This is a wireless Cricut machine usually used to cut paper, fabric, and even more. It also works with the Circuit Design Space app.

. . .

The Cricut Explore Air 2

Being an upgrade to the Cricut Air, this Cricut machine cuts about twice as fast as the Cricut Air. The Cricut Explore comes in various colors and works with the current Circuit Design Space app.

The Cricut Explore one

Similar in appearance and representation to the other Explore machines, this Cricut Explore one is a handy Cricut machine. Still, this Cricut machine has a single tool holder. You can also cut and write with this Cricut machine, but you must do it in two passes.

Cricut Explore Air

The Cricut Explore, Explore Air, and Explore Air 2 all feature dual tool holders, so you can use them to write and cut in one pass. The Explore has a single tool holder so it can write and cut in two passes.

The Explore Air and Explore Air 2 usually feature built-in Bluetooth, but for the Explore One and Explore Cricut machines, you'll need a Cricut wireless Bluetooth adapter to use with iOS or your Android mobile device or just cut wirelessly from your computer.

Cricut Expression 2

The Cricut Expression 2 was designed primarily as a standalone type of machine. And the LCD touch screen and Cricut® cartridges allow you to create different projects without even being connected to a computer. Usually, a computer is needed to update the machine's firmware.

A Cricut Expression Machine

The Cricut Expression machine had several great features available. A couple of favorites are the AutoFill and Quantity features. They allowed you to cut multiples of an equivalent image so you could quickly create a batch of invitations, place settings, party favors, or other projects. There was a scoring tip that would be used.

The Cricut Mini Machine:

Cricut Mini Machine is based solely on the use of the Cricut Craft Room, a computer program that no longer uses features. Circuit Mini is characterized by being obsolete.

The Cricut Imagine

The Cricut Imagine machine uses a special cutting mat with a white border and a black registration mark. The Cricut machine will read before cutting precisely the chosen images. The Imagine machine was not able to read the other types of mats.

The Cricut Cake

The Cricut cake machine is specially designed to cut edible material, such as gum paste, sheets of icing, and more. As such, the Cricut cake machine was designed with several parts made from food-safe material. Any part of this machine that touches food was made from food-safe material.

The Cricut Create

The Cricut Create machine was primarily designed to work with Cricut cartridges as a standalone machine.

DESIGN SPACE TOOL

Design Space is considered a cloud-based design software that is characterized by being lightweight and easy to learn. Use this app whenever inspiration strikes you, and you can take advantage of its compatibility that extends from Mac to Android devices and iOs. You can even use it offline.

Cricut Design Space could also be a complementary app that allows you to improve and cut wirelessly with the Cricut Explore and Cricut Maker machines. With the help of a Cricut Design Space, you can create a project or browse thousands of pictures and images.

Have you simply recognized your Cricut machine and aren't sure what to do next? This is often where you will learn the basics of Design Space for beginners to use with all Cricut machines.

The Cricut Design Space is usually designed in a way that this program will have to choose, design, and customize designs; then, all you have to do is send the designs and images to your Cricut to cut it. This tutorial is usually used for all brands of Cricut machines.

Before you get started, join Design.Cricut.com and download the software to your computer. Or download the app to your device. Create a design space account, and you're all set!

The design space has two main components: the house page and the canvas. The home page is where you discover new and saved projects. Canvas is where you will organize or project your projects.

HOME PAGE OF A DESIGN SPACE

When you open the design space, the first page you see is the home page. The home page has four important parts: the header, the banner, your projects, and the featured content.

THE 4 PARTS OF THE HOME PAGE

If you're a beginner and want to use a Cricut design space, you should start with a very detailed tutorial on where each tool is, and then you can use it.

1. a header
2. a banner
3. your projects
4. ready to do projects

1. **A HEADER**

The menu icon is also called hamburger, and this allows you to switch between the home page and then the canvas. The menu contains Cricut machine configuration, specific calibration, different account details, cartridge connection, Cricut access, and help. The Miscellaneous Settings tab allows you to pack the grid into the design space or adjust the displayed units.

1. **A SCROLL**

This carousel area scrolls some slides to the foreground. This is often where new information, special offers, maintenance announcements, or new products will be featured here.

1. **MY PROJECTS**

This is where your projects are displayed, sorted by last opened. Click on view all to look at them all. This is often where you'll scroll to look for a selected project.

1. **READY TO DO PROJECTS**

The following few banners will allow you to make projects sorted by category. Some examples of this step include various projects included with Cricut Access, projects from the material or machine.

CANVAS

You can access the Canvas from 3 different areas on the homepage, on which you can click the Cricut design of the app. There are three different areas with toolbars within the Canvas area. The header, the planning panel, and the layers toolbar:

PANEL LAYERS

The various layers of the Cricut cutting machine panel will help show each element on its r of your designs. Choosing the color of each layer you are looking for is very important because it groups each layer of equivalent paint on an equivalent cutting mat.

Each design looks like green-teal with cutouts on an equivalent piece of paper. Layers allow you to adjust the parts individually and alter their line type (whether they cut, draw, emboss, etc.). If you had a paper that could also have a shape cut out as a scoreline, you would want the cardboard, scoreline, and cut out all on an equivalent layer and stuck together.

HEADER

The header of the Cricut design space typically contains the menu, the project name, the machine selection menu, and the Green Make it button. Always be sure to choose which machine you will use to make the right menu and gear options available to you.

TEXT

Add some words and phrases to the drawing area. And when text is added, the Edit Text toolbar will be displayed. You can then inspect the simpler Cricut design fonts.

MODELS

The various templates in the design space will also give you a reference for size and scale. The image won't be cropped, and it will just show you on the canvas how big your shirt or item to customize is so you can resize your design accordingly.

PROJECTS

Search for project ideas and prepare completed projects. Projects are often divided into various categories, including project types, seasons, or events. Examples usually include featured Cricut access projects, Christmas, ink infused, blade, iron-on, planners, and sewing.

UPLOAD

Cut your images by uploading .jpg, .gif, .png, .bmp, .svg or .dxf files for free use. Here is a tutorial for more details about how to upload your image and how to download svg.

DESIGN PANEL

This design panel will open a replacement blank canvas page in the design space app.

IMAGES

With the help of this feature, you can select; browse; then insert different images from the Cricut Browse image library. You can also include your uploaded pictures and on the canvas.

SHAPES

Add basic shapes such as circles, squares, triangles, and features to the canvas. There are tons of personal effects you can do to shape and customize your designs using basic shapes. You can then incorporate the different details that into another tutorial.

CRICUT DESIGN TOOLS

Are you looking to customize designs in the design space? Once you feel ready, you'll learn everything you need to know about Cricut design spaces and tools. You can shape, flatten, weld, group, and contour.

THE TOOL I NEED

After talking about Cricut and what you can do with this revolutionary machine, what kind of tools do you need for your Cricut machine to start working, and how can you use them? When you start creating different projects with Cricut, you'll find that you'll want tools to make your life easier. You can always buy the right tools in smaller packages, but it's also important to have an essential toolset that groups the different tools. Generally, the Cricut Essential toolset comes with several tools and a scoring blade, and an additional replacement blade for the trimmer. And here are the most important tools you should have with Cricut that you can't work with without its help:

A CRICUT CUTTING MAT

These are some must-have tools, regardless of the type of Cricut you're using and regardless of the types of projects, you plan to cut using the Cricut machine. Cricut has several different mat options; they are color-coded, so it can make creating and designing your projects easier for you.

AN XACTO KNIFE

To properly use a Cricut machine, you should have a xacto knife; it will be useful for your various Cricut projects. Xacto makes one of the most versatile tools you should have in your craft rooms. You can choose to use the xacto knife when you de-sketch your designs overusing your Cricut de-sketching tool. And they are considered an inexpensive tool that you can pick and choose anywhere. You can also use this knife to cut small dots in any design you choose during the cutting process.

A TRANSFER TAPE

A transfer tape is generally very useful and helpful for various vinyl-type projects. We can define this transfer tape as a specific form of a backing sheet that can help you get your chosen vinyl design from the paper stock you use; then, on the base, you place it on it. And although it may be a bit challenging to decide which transfer tape will be the best fit, here's a tip that can help you, there is a stringer and high tack transfer tape that is considered perfect for permanent grade vinyl. And it takes a stronger tack to lift the vinyl material off the paper backing you choose to use. In addition, the stenciling material can also be easily removed from its paper backing more easily because the tack is not that stringy like permanent grade vinyl.

A CARDBOARD

Cardstock is a must-have tool that you should keep in any craft space or room. And it's wonderful to create your own set of beautifully presented cardstock designs. Creating a large number of cardstock is not just meant for the purpoo many cards. The cardstock you should use should be thicker than the usual type of paper. This cardstock can be used to cut out different shapes and forms on wood, so all you have to do is cut with a saw to get the shapes you want to have.

SCISSORS

Scissors are a must-have tool that you can't work on creating in general without using them. And in general, scissors are considered an indispensable craft tool that you can't give up using with different materials. You can use scissors for papercrafts, vinyl heat transfer, fabric, or any other type of material.

GROUPED VINYL

Vinyl, there are some unique alternatives here. I won't dive too deeply into their disparities, but you can use vinyl for various designs and uses: shirt designs, decals on vehicles and mugs or cups, creating signs, naming your warehouse, and more. You can also purchase packages of various types of vinyl. This is an amazing method to have something available simply on the off chance that you have the sooty need to do something that requires a particular type of vinyl.

A VINYL SQUEEGEE

This tool is generally used when you want to apply vinyl, but you can also use it so you can smooth out different types of paper projects. There are several sizes that you can purchase this tool. You use all kinds of squeegees. For example, you can use the vinyl squeegee to make wooden signs and use them for other projects.

AN ADHESIVE TAPE

This is a must-have tool you'll need to use for your Cricut machine, and you'll need it to do any kind of papermaking. Duct tape is very easy and simple to use and offers a preferable and wide range of uses. There are some distinct alternatives for duct tape out there. Pretty much the same as with anything ranging from very reasonable to a bit more expensive.

ONE GREEN MAT: A STANDARD POCKET: use

to cut any heavy cardstock or iron on, vinyl, and even more types of material

A BLUE PAPER - A LIGHTWEIGHT POCKET: You can use it with standard paper, vellum, light cardstock, and even more

A PINK MOP - A FABRIC POCKET: This type of carpet is used to cut most fabric types with the help of a rotating blade or an adhesive cloth blade.

A PURPLE MAT - A STRONG TAKE: Use a mat board, special cardstock, and backing fabric.

You can, for example, use a green mat for your projects or a purple e mat depending on your preference and taste.

CRICUT MACHINE TWEEZERS:

This specific tool is a great tool that you can use to get those little pieces of your chosen design.

MARKERS

Rather than creating a cutting design with your Cricut machine, you can also write with your Cricut using these Cricut pens. With these markers, you can accomplish a wide range of tasks, including creating personalized coloring sheets for your kids. You can also use a pen connector with your Cricut cutting machine.

PORTABLE TRIMMER:

Using a portable trimmer can help you get precise and straight lines. Using this tool, you can cut the edges of the vinyl so that they line up perfectly on the mat.

This tool usually comes with a scoring blade or a spare blade.

THE CRICUT SCRAPER TOOL

The Cricut scraper tool is usually used to clean and remove any unwanted scraps from your cutting mat. This tool is very useful and can help you whenever you have sophisticated cutting tasks and have a million small pieces stuck to your cutting mat. You can also use it for sanding your vinyl when you put it on.

A CRICUT SCORING STYLUS.

In general, the stylus is considered very useful and important to produce some neat folding lines. It is also inserted into the slot of your machine.

A CRICUT SQUEEGEE:

The Cricut spatula is very useful for lifting several images from the cutting mat. You can use a Cricut squeegee whenever you have an intricate cut that you don't want to risk ruining or tearing the image.

CRICUT DISSOLVER:

This tool is very important if you want to remove any small cuts. You can use this tool for any type of small vinyl text. You may never realize how small those pieces are.

There is an additional handy accessory that you can have for your Cricut machine, and that is the accessory case. You should always keep all your tools all together in one place and where you can use them. You can also store your tools by zipping them up.

MAKER TOOLS

Every crafter has a distinctive approach to bringing their ideas to life, and you may want to supplement your artistic tools by employing one or more of the tools listed below to create extraordinary projects.

Wavy Blade - The "Wavy blade" will help you create decorative edges much faster than a drag blade for a wide range of projects with smoothly shaped cuts. This uniquely designed stainless steel blade is perfect for creating "original vinyl decals, iron-on designs, envelopes, cards, gift tags, and collage projects," or when you're looking to add elegant accents with a whimsical wavy edge to your craft. It is recommended for use with "iron on iron, vinyl, paper, cardstock, and fabric." This blade can only be used with the "Cricut Maker" machine.

Fine Debossing Tip - The "Fine Debossing Tip" (2.0 mm) is the ultimate tool for creating elegant papercrafts by incorporating professional finishes and elevation to the base material. It will help you achieve crisp designs with fine detail. This tip is uniquely designed with a "rotating debossing ball," which will provide you with the freedom to create custom and personalized designs with exceptional complexity, unlike the standard "embossing folders" available in the market that limit you in a predefined layout. You can easily create dimensional wedding cards, monogrammed thank you notes, or flourishes attached to gift boxes and gift tags, and much more. You can also create a stunning effect on "coated paper, glittery and glittery paper and foil cardstock." This tip can only be used with the "Cricut Maker" machine. It is recommended to use "cardstock, aluminum poster board, aluminum cardstock, aluminum kraft board, poster board, and kraft board."

Engraving Tip - The "Cricut Engraving Tip" will help you generate custom text and monograms. You can design ornamental embellishments and flourishes and inscribe any famous quote of your choice on a keepsake. This tip is made with high-quality carbide steel that will allow engraving on "Cricut Aluminum Sheets" and anodized aluminum so that you can highlight the silver underneath for a professional-looking effect. This tip can only be used with the "Cricut Maker" machine. The "Cricut Engraving Tip" will help you create intricate custom engraved plates, personalized nameplates, engraved art and decor, jewelry, monograms, wood carvings, and keepsakes. It is recommended to use "flat aluminum, soft metals, leather, acrylic, plastic," among others.

Basic Perforation Blade - The "Basic Perforation Blade" is uniquely designed with "2.5mm teeth and 0.5mm gaps" to quickly generate smooth rips with accurate and consistent perforation cuts for all your craft projects. For all your perforated design needs, this blade will allow you to create patterns with finely perforated, uniform lines that would eliminate the need to fold the paper before ripping and is very useful, especially for shapes with curves. You can effortlessly create "torn pamphlet pages, raffle tickets, homemade journals" or any project that requires neat tearing, such as Christmas decorations, paper dolls, torn cards or gift certificates, advent calendars, and more. It is recommended for use with "fabrics such as paper, cardstock, foam, acetate, and foil." This blade can only be used with the "Cricut Maker" machine.

PENS

"Cricut" offers a range of pens to help you get flawless and eye-catching handwritten texts to create custom invitations, banners, gift tags for cards, among others. A wide variety of pens can be used with both the "Cricut Maker" and "Cricut Explore" lines, so you can cut and write with ease. Most pens are "acid-free, non-toxic, and permanent" once the text has dried. Some of the "Cricut Pens" that you can purchase are listed below:

- "Cricut Explore Metallic Pen Set" contains five pens, each in gold, silver, copper, blue and purple.

- "Fine Point Pen Set, Wisteria," contains 5 0.4 point pens in Magenta, Fawn, Light Green, Turquoise, and Light Turquoise.
- "Gel Pen Set, Metallic Dark Petals," contains five medium points (1.0) pens in Dusty Pink, Plum, Green, Black, Silver.
- "Gel Pen Set, Peacock," contains five fine point pens (1pt) in Aqua, Purple, Dark Gray, Pink, Teal.
- "Glitter Gel Pen Set, Fiesta," contains five medium points (0.8) pens in Scarlet Red, Dark Brown, Orange, Kelly Green, Tawny.
- "Glitter Gel Pen Set, Mermaid," which ns five medium-point pens (0.8) in Plum, Peacock, Dark Pink, Olive, Bordeaux.
- "Gel Pen Set, Fingerpaint," which contain medium-point pens (1.0) in Orange, Lime, Red, Yellow, Blue.
- "Extra Fine Point Pen Set, Spring Rain," which contain extra-fine point pens (0.3) in Gray, Mint, Raspberry, Peacock, Lilac.
- "Extra Fine Point Pen Set, Bohemian," which contain extra-fine point pens (0.3) in Raspberry, Teal, Burnt Orange, Plum, Dark Green.
- "Pen Set, Antiquity" contains five pens in

Jade, Wine, Crystal Pink, Gemstone Blue, and Midnight.

- "Variety Pen/Marker Set, Martha Stewart Spring Bouquet," which contains three fine point pens (0.4) in Crystal Pink, Cactus Pink, Sage along with two medium point markers (1.0) in Gold, Silver.
- "Extra Fine Point Pen Set, Martha Stewart Gilded Forest" contains five extra-fine point pens (0.3) in dark green, black, dark blue, brown, gray.
- "Ultimate Fine Point Pen Set" which contains 30 different Fine Point pens (0.4 points) in "Black, Red, Blue, Green, Yellow, Bitter Apple, Candy Corn, Cornflower, Candy Crystal, Tres Berry, Pink Cactus, Bluebonnet, Lavender, Honeysuckle, Sage, Armadillo, Geode, Indian Red, Adobe Clay, Moccasin, Jade, Gemstone Blue, Wine, Pink Crystal, Coral, Turquoise, Tawny, Light Green, Light Turquoise and Magenta."

Infusible Ink Pens

"Infusible Ink Markers" will allow you to create intricate freehand designs, or you can use any of your "Cricut" machines to create custom designs on plain laser copy paper. All pens are "acid-free, water-based, and ASTM D-4236 compliant". They are available in many colors and in two-line weights, which upon heat transfer, resulting in deep, vibrant colors. This will not flake, peel, wrinkle or crack. These pens are suitable for use with the "Cricut Maker" and "Cricut Explore" lines and require "Infusible Ink blanks" and compatible heat presses that can reach a temperature of 400°F (205°C). You'll be able to design custom designs and text for baby bodysuits, t-shirts, bags, coasters, and more. Unlike the "iron-on or vinyl" application, where designs must be plated onto a base material with adhesive, the "Infusible Ink" heat transfer is fused into the material itself. Some of the "Infusible Ink" pens available for purchase from "Michaels" include:

"Infusible Ink Markers (1.0), Basics," which contains five medium points (1.0) markers in Cardinal, Black, Ultraviolet, Tawny, Bright Green.

"Infusible Ink Markers (0.4), Basics," which contains five fine points (0.4) Infusible Ink™ pens in Cardinal, Black, Ultraviolet, Tawny, Bright Green.

"Infusible Ink Markers (1.0), Neons," which contains five medium points (1.0) markers in Neon Pink, Neon Blue, Neon Orange, Neon Yellow, Neon Green.

"Infusible Ink Markers (0.4), Neons," which contains five fine point (0.4) pens in Neon Pink, Neon Blue, Neon Orange, Neon Yellow, Neon Green.

CRAFTING TOOLS

"Cricut" also offers various crafting tools such as rulers, fabric shears, seam rippers, thread shears, knives, trimmers, rotary cutters, measuring tape, and more. All tools are carefully designed to help you take your crafting skills to the next level, resulting in professional-looking crafts with premium finishes. For example, the "True Control Knife Kit" contains five replacement blades along with a storage cartridge to help you track and discard used blades. This knife is designed with a razor-sharp edge, piercing tip. Top blade lock system "to give you better control and amazing finish every time. It can be used to create precision cuts on paper, cardstock, thin plastic, canvas, and various other materials. Their "patented hands-free blade change system" means you can safely change your blades without having to touch them and accidentally injure yourself. It also boasts an "anti-roll design" to ensure the knife stays in place when not in use along with a padded handle for a comfortable handling experience.

STORAGE

There are three different categories of storage bags specifically designed for "Cricut" machines and tools as described below:

EasyPress Tote - These bags are specifically designed for storing the "Cricut EasyPress" along with its safety base, mat, and other small accessories at home or on the go. They are made of sturdy, heat-resistant material to protect your device from bumps and scratches while working through heat transfer projects. A comfortable shoulder strap and powerful grip handle will allow for easy carrying with the Velcro strap to secure the device for travel. A back pocket and front pocket are added for storing iron mats and accessories.

Machine Bags - These premium storage bags are 26" long, 9.25" wide, and 9.25" high and carefully designed so you can organize and store your "Cricut" machine at home and easily transport it if needed. The bag has side pockets and compartments to store tools and craft supplies and comes with a sturdy double snap handle. These bags have soft padding to provide additional protection and shock absorption. You can purchase these bags in different colors (purple, navy, tweed, and raspberry).

Rolling Craft Tote - These bags feature rollers for easy portability and storage at home. They are 26" long, 10.25" wide, and 14.38" tall, but remember that these bags are designed to store your craft supplies and will not fit on any "Cricut" machines. These bags are also available in several colors (Purple, Navy, Tweed, and Raspberry).

MACHINE MATS

There are three different categories of mats offered

by "Cricut" compatible with different "Cricut" machines and hot presses, as described below:

The "StandardGrip Machine Mat" is 12 x 12 inches and compatible with all "Circuit" machines. These mats are designed to hold the material firmly while cutting and then easily remove the material when ready. They are recommended for use with "cardstock, patterned paper, embossed cardstock, iron-on, and vinyl."

They also offer "LightGrip Machine Mat," which is 12 x 12 inches and specifically designed to adhere to lightweight, delicate materials such as "standard paper, lightweight cardstock, and vellum."

Their "StrongGrip Machine Mat" comes in 12 x 24 inches and serves as a sturdy adhesion surface for heavy materials, including "thick cardstock, glitter board, magnetic material, chipboard, poster board and fabric (with stabilizer)." The company says these mats are their "most durable mat with dual-life adhesive technology."

The "**FabricGrip Machine Mat**" is available in 12 x 12 inches and 12 x 24 inches is designed with high-density PVC for added strength and coated with light-weight adhesive for easy use with various fabrics such as "silk, canvas, leather, and cotton."

Self-Healing Mats - "Cricut" offers a wide vamanyling mats and claims they are twice as self-healing as their competitors. They are designed with larger numbers on a 1" wide border for easy readability. These mats cannot be used inside "Cricut" machines. Some of these offerings include "Self-Care Decorative Mat, Mint," "Self-Care Mat, Blue," "Self-Care Decorative Mat, Lilac," and more.

EasyPress Mats - The "Cricut EasyPress Mat" is uniquely designed to work with "Cricut EasyPress" for flawless heat transfer projects. The long-lasting cover provides uniform heat conduction and even heat distribution. Inner lining can easily absorb moisture resulting in clean, dry heat. The foil membrane can reflect heat onto the material, preventing moisture vapor transfer while the silicone foam insulates the surface and protects it from heat damage. They are available in 3 different sizes, namely, 12 x 12 inches, 20 x 16 inche,s and 8 x 10 inch,es and special "Decorative Polka Dot Mats in blue/mint and pink/lilac" in 14 x 14 inches.

CRICUT CUTTLEBUG MACHINE

The "Cricut Cuttlebug" is a machine for cutting and embossing a range of different materials. With clean, crisp cuts and even deep embossing for professional quality results. "Cricut" also offers a full line of compatible "Cuttlebug embossing folders and cutting mantles," while you can still use other folders and dies offered by other leading brands. You can use this machine in addition to cutting and embossing paper but also for a variety of other materials, including "tissue paper, foils, acetate tape, and thin leather." A variety of accessories for this material are also offered, including cutting spacers and embossing folders.

CRICUT BRIGHTPAD

The "Cricut BrightPad" is an electronic crafting pad that looks like a tablet. You can use it to brighten up your paper designs to make it easier to draw, tracing, disentangling, quilt, and reduce eye strain in the process. It is thin, light, and sturdy for comfortable use and portability, with 9 x 11.5 inches of the evenly LED illuminated area and five different brightness settings. It is made of "6H Hardness Surface", which makes it highly scratch-resistant. You can use it for diffing vinyl or iron-on designs and paper cake quilt blocks. Bas as well as for patterns, jewelry, needlepoint.

CHAPTER TWO

THE CRICUT MAINTENANCE: DO IT EASY

CRICUT BLADES MAINTENANCE AND CARE

USE YOUR BLADES WITH RECOMMENDED MATERIALS

THE LIFE of your blades can be decreased in case you

are not using your blades properly and as recommended. While you need to get a hold of which mat to use for which type of material by yourself, as Design Space doesn't recommend appropriate mats, Design Space will help you choose suitable blades based on the material you are using for your crafting project. Moreover, you need to make sure that the right blade is used on the material you are cutting as you can damage the blade in case you choose to cut the wrong type of material. Follow the advice from Design Space and make sure that each of your blades is used on an appropriate material or fabric.

PROTECT THE BLADES AND HOUSING GEARS

Quick Swap Scoring Wheel and blades for Cricut machines all have plastic covers. Make sure to keep these covers and use them to protect your blades when not in use. By properly storing your blades, you are protecting your tools from outside particles that can compromise the functionality of your tools, such as dust. The plastic cover protects blades and housing gears at the same time.

STORE YOUR BLADES PROPERLY

When you are not using your blades, make sure to cover them and store them properly. You can keep your tools in a storage pouch or a box. Blades can be safely kept in your Cricut machine. The machine is designed to provide storage for the blades you are not using, while the storage compartment also has a magnet to keep your blades neatly stored. You can keep your tools in the Cricut machine storage compartment as well. This way, you will always have all the blades and tools you need, accessible whenever you want to use them, but also protected and safe from damage.

HOW TO CLEAN A CRICUT MACHINE
DO NOT USE SCRAPPER

With the pink Fabric Grip mat, there is no need to use the scrapper because the adhesive on it is different from the others and can be scraped off the mat.

KEEP YOUR HANDS OFF

Unlike other mats, the Cricut pink mat is made with delicate adhesive. Thus, if your hands are oily, they can easily break down the adhesive on the mat, resulting in the loss of its stickiness.

Be very careful with the mat and try as much as possible to avoid touching the adhesive. To adhere your fabric to the mat, use a Brayer, and do not apply too much force, just enough to get you to stick to the mat. Another way of keeping your hands off the mat is by using Tweezers to pick up pieces of materials from it. Desist from picking up a loose thread from the mat—use Tweezers if you really must pick.

THREADS

Talking about threads, whenever you cut the fabric, you'll realize that you end up with a lot of threads on the mat. Leave them. In our minds, we believe that our mats have to be super clean because any form of a bump when cutting vinyl or paper can be detrimental to our project. However, the rotary blade is super awesome, it can cut through loose threads even if there is fabric over it.

SAVE THE PINK MAT FOR FABRIC

You can opt to back your felt in transfer tape and stick that to the mat. You just have to peel it off after the cut. Depending on the material you're cutting, this option can be capital intensive because you'll be using transfer tape for every cut.

DO NOT RE-STICK THE MAT

On the internet, there are so many tutorials on how to re-stick the Cricut mat, and they involve the use of baby wipes, water, painter's tape, Goo Gone, spray adhesive and many others. However, you have to understand that the pink mat's adhesive is completely different from the adhesive on other mats, and if you use any of those materials to re-stick it, you'll end up damaging your pink mat. The pink mat's adhesive is designed to grip fabric, but also release it easily.

HOW TO MAKE YOUR CUTTING MAT STICKY AGAIN

After washing or cleaning your cutting mat, you have to make them sticky again. The most advisable way to make your mat sticky again is by adding glue to it. Get a solid glue stick like the Zig 2-Way Glue Pen and apply it to the mat's inner part. Then, stroke the glue around the mat and make sure no glue remains on the edges of the mat.

After about 30 minutes, the glue will turn clear. If the cutting mat turns out to be too sticky after applying glue, you can use a piece of fabric to reduce the adhesive by pressing the material on the parts of the mat that are very sticky. Cover the mat with a clear film cover after a few hours. You can also use tacky glues or spray adhesives that are ideal for cutting mats.

GENERAL MAINTENANCE

When your mat isn't in use, cover it with a clear film cover so that dust and hairs won't accumulate on the mat's surface.

Handle your mats with care. If you want to ensure that the adhesive does not get damaged, avoid touching the sticky surface with your hands.

Always ensure that your mat dries entirely before using it or covering it up. Don't use heat when drying your mat, but you can place it in front of a fan. Also, ensure that it is drying hanging up so that both sides will dry.

CHAPTER THREE

DESIGN SPACE: HOW TO SET UP YOUR FIRST CUSTOM PROJECT

WITH DESIGN SPACE, there are unlimited possibilities. Depending on the cutting machine, some of the older design cartridges can still be used with the software. Design Space has a library full of preloaded designs, templates and images. You are not limited to using Design Space or Cricut images either. You can also upload your own images.

GETTING STARTED WITH CRICUT DESIGN SPACE

Once you have downloaded Design Space, you will find it easy to learn the program. Design Space costs nothing to download and install. Although there are some designs, images and fonts that are charged to your account, there are many free images, templates, shapes and fonts.

Once you have a Design Space ID, you have access to the software's vast library of designs and all of its cutting capabilities. Design Space offers a limited-time free trial of Cricut Access, which is a membership-based library of images, designs, projects and more.

The great thing about Design Space is that you do not have to have a Cricut Access membership to buy any of the projects, images, or designs. You can purchase them if and when you require them.

CRICUT DESIGN SPACE QUICK GUIDE

There are two main screens for Design Space.

HOME SCREEN

This is the first screen you will encounter when Design Space loads. You can click on any of the project windows in each section to access or view the projects.

The screen is split into the following sections:

- Top Menu Bar—This is the top, dark gray Menu bar. When you are on the Canvas screen, this menu bar will have the following options on it:

- Home—This indicates the screen you are viewing.
- Welcome <Name> message—This will have your login name.
- My Projects—This will take you to the directory of your stored/saved projects.
- Machine—This is the cutting machine selection menu. The minute you have selected your default machine, the machine will be loaded every time you log in.
- "New Project" button—This will send you to a clean Canvas screen to begin working on a new project.
- My Projects—This will list all of your current projects.
- Cricut Access—This will list the latest ready-to-make projects from Cricut Access.
- My Ready-to-Make Projects—This section selects ready-to-make projects for you, based on your latest projects.
- Other promotional sections—There are a few sections that display the latest projects and materials available to you.

CANVAS SCREEN

This is the Design Screen where you will create all of your projects.

The Canvas screen is split into the following sections:

- Top Menu Bar—This is the top, dark gray Menu bar. When you are on the Canvas screen, this menu bar will have the following options on it:
- Canvas—This indicates the screen you are viewing.
- Untitled—This will remain "Untitled" until you have saved your current project. If you load a saved project, it will list the name of the opened project.
- My Projects—This will take you to the directory of your stored/saved projects.
- Save—This is the save button for your project. Once a project has been saved, there will be a second option listed "Save As." The "Save As" option is there so you can save a project as another name and keep the current one intact.
- Machine—This is the cutting machine selection menu. Once you have selected your default machine, it will load every time you log in.

- "Make it" button—This button sends your current project to the "Prepare" screen to ready your design for cutting.
- Top Drop-down Menu Bar — (3 stripes in the top left-hand corner of the gray menu bar).
- The Design Panel—This is the selection panel on the left-hand side of the screen. Sometimes, it is simply called the left-hand menu. The Design Panel is where you can select the object you are going to use for your design projects. These objects include Templates, Projects, Images, Text, Shapes and an option to upload your own designs.
- Edit Menu—This menu can be found below the top gray menu bar. It should be noted that.
- Arrange—This arranges the order of the objects.
- Flip—This "Flips" the object either vertically or horizontally. It also rotates it by 90°.
- Size—This option resizes the selected image(s).
- Rotate—This option allows you to rotate objects to a certain angle. It allows for some interesting object positioning on the screen.
- Position—This will place a selected object at the desired coordinates.

- The Layers and Color Sync panel—This is the panel found on the right-hand side of the Canvas screen. It is broken into two tabs.
- Layers tab—The Layers tab has a menu with the following options at the top:
- Group—Objects that need to be kept together on the screen to be moved, marked, colored, etc. are easier to work with when they are grouped.
- Ungroup—Ungroup is grayed out until objects have been grouped. Ungroup disconnects Grouped objects.
- Duplicate—This option is used to clone selected objects and make an exact replica of them.
- Delete—This option is used to delete selected objects.
- Color Sync tab—This tab is useful when you have objects that you want to be drawn or printed in the exact same color. It will list the exact colors of all the objects on the screen for you to match other objects with.
- Canvas Objects—The panel beneath the Layers panel menu lists all the objects currently on the design screen. As you get more familiar with working in Design Space, you will find this panel very useful.

- Bottom Menu of the Layers/Color Sync panel—The bottom section of this panel has the following options:
- Canvas—This hides or unhides any embedded objects on the Canvas, such as templates or background color.
- Slice—This is for slicing up an object on the canvas.
- Weld—Welds two objects together to form an outline.
- Attach—Attaches objects on the screen that need to be printed together.
- Flatten—Flattens an image with multiple parts into a single image.
- The Design Canvas—This is the graphed space in the middle of the screen where you will do all of your designs. It is set in inches as a default, but the settings can be customized through the top right-hand Drop-down menu.
- At the bottom right-hand corner of the Canvas is the Zoom Control. This is grayed out until you hover the mouse cursor over it. By default, it is set to 100% scale. You can set it to zoom in or out of the screen by using the + and - selection icons on each side of the current zoom % marker.

PREPARE SCREEN

This is a screen that you will get to when you are ready to start cutting the project and have pressed the "Make it" button.

- Top Gray Menu—The Drop-down menu on the left of this menu only has one option when you are at the "Prepare" screen, which is to take you back to the Canvas. The name of the menu changes to "Prepare," and next to the name, you will see the number of machine mat changes the project requires (1 mat). There will be the name of the project and the name of the cutting machine.

The left-hand panel has the following options:

- Project copies—This must not be confused with the number of cuts. This option will duplicate the design objects according to the amount selected.
- Small Mat image—Depending on the number of machine mats required for the project, you could see a number of these small mats. This is where you select the mat you want to edit, rearrange, etc. Next to the mat, it will tell you

if the machine is going to cut or draw the object. It may also indicate if the object is to be printed.
- Material Size—Here you can select the material size. This helps to cut down on using unnecessary material.
- Mirror—The sliding button next to this option will turn mirroring on or off. Mirroring turns the objects on the mat upside down.
- Machine Mats—In the middle of the screen, you will find an exact replica of the machine mat and how the design is placed to be cut. You can move objects around the screen to position them for cutting.
- Cancel button—In the bottom right-hand corner of the screen, you will find the "Cancel" button. This button will cancel the cut and return you to the Design Canvas screen.
- Continue button—The "Continue" button is in the bottom right-hand corner of the screen. This takes the cutting to the next stage. You will be prompted to load the accessories in the cutting machine, select the material being used and load the machine mat.

CHAPTER FOUR

TIPS AND TRICKS ON HOW TO CREATE CANVAS

THERE'RE SO many amazing shortcuts that Cricut users can use to make their work faster and organized. However, if these shortcuts are not known, there is no way they can be applied. If all users knew how they could make use of some tools and functions in a very efficient way, then maybe they wouldn't have to spend so much time on every project.

All the information I'm about to share in this section is majorly from experiences gained from making use of the Design Space over the years. Therefore, this is not just some random tips and techniques from a novice or cheap source. Let's get right on with it, shall we?

This section will be divided into two categories; the design canvas platform and the cut screen platform.

THE DESIGN CANVAS PLATFORM

The following are ways you can work smarter on the design canvas platform:

MAKING USE OF CARTRIDGE FOR SEARCHING SIMILAR IMAGES: Most times, the numerous outcomes of images gotten from the search bar in the image library can overwhelm a Cricut user. Whenever an image is searched, too many dissimilar results pop up. It, most of the time, makes it difficult to single out one favorite image out of these results. And sometimes, when a favorite image is found, more similar images are always wanted. To stop this from happening again, ensure that you make use of the cartridge of the image you're searching for. The easiest and fastest means of accessing a cartridge of an image is by clicking the small information (i) icon that is located at the bottom right of the image on the Design Space image library. By doing that, the image's details will be revealed. A green link will also appear, giving you access to every image of equal similarity. Knowing this will enable you to start matching or coordinating images, which is more effective than the outcomes from the search bar.

CUTTING, DRAWING, OR SCORING LINES: In the past, Cricut users had to search for designs that had specific attributes for drawing and scoring a line (instead of cutting). Not anymore, those days are behind all Cricut users. With the latest upgrade that has been made by Cricut on the Design Space, a user can comfortably change lines from cutting to drawing to scoring by merely making use of the easy-to-use "Line type" menu positioned at the topmost toolbar.

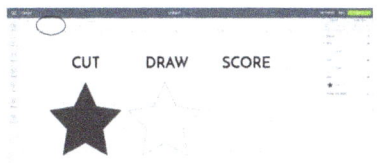

COLOR MANAGEMENT: If you can maximize the use of the "Color Synchronization" tool, you can significantly save much time working on different projects. This will likely ensure that you are using colors that match various designs. A lot of times, when you work on a lot of designs on the Design canvas simultaneously, you may end up with several shades of similar colors. Instead of choosing all the single layers autonomously to recolor, go to the "Color Sync" tool positioned on the tool panel on the right side. The colors you will find on this panel are the ones that are presently in use. Notwithstanding, you can also drag active layers that are currently on the design by using your mouse and dropping it in a new color that hasn't been used on the design. If you desire to maintain the use of matching colors throughout your project designs, or you wish to have some layers with the same color to cut more efficiently, making use of the "Color Sync" is the fastest and most comfortable way of doing it.

APPLYING THE HIDE TOOL: A lot of users find themselves crowding the Canvas area with too many redundant images while they work on their projects. And they end up cutting all the elements on the Canvas area when the time comes to cut out their projects. There're likewise some times when you will wish or have to cut out some portions of the design you're working on. Instead of getting these unnecessary images deleted off your canvas screen, you can just hide them by clicking the little eye icon positioned by the right side of the Layers panel beside the image. You should note that any image you hide won't be permanently disconnected from the Canvas. However, it will not be added with the rest of the images when moving your project for cutting. You may also toggle the Hide icon on/off. This will make it easier to cut the parts needed only, and also keep an organized and clean Design canvas at the same time, without getting the images you still want to work on mixed up.

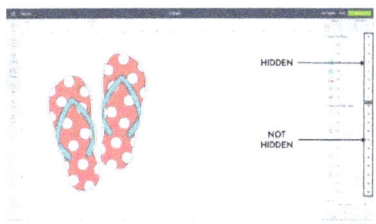

ADJUST IMAGE PATTERNS: The Fill tool located at the topmost toolbar allows you to modify the way you fill images. Picking a single layer from the panel, colors can be switched, or the interior of the image can be given a different pattern.

There're quite a lot of pre-loaded patterns that can be used to fill images to make the project more stimulating without having to depend on patterned scrapbooks or cardstock. Even though there're numerous designs to choose from, the scale and orientation of the chosen pattern can also be altered by clicking "Edit Pattern" located in the "Pattern" menu under the Fill pane. It is important to note that you can only use this function through the "Print then Cut" method.

THE CUT SCREEN PLATFORM

A lot of Cricut users tend to think they won't be able to go further with their project editing once they send it for cutting after designing. They believe the editing ends immediately after clicking on the "Make It" button. But there're still so many actions and editing that a user can carry out on the "Cut Screen" platform. And if done wisely, you will be able to save a lot of time and spare some materials.

By making these adjustments, you won't only be able to make your work more perfect than the default settings would make it, you will also have your cut wherever and however you desire it. Your project looks better with these adjustments, especially when you're working on a scrap or an oddly shaped material. Just make sure that your Cut screen gridlines are fit into the gridlines of your mat to ensure that your design fits the material correctly wherever it is placed.

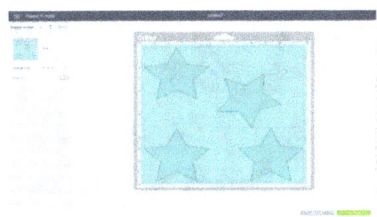

MOVING IMAGES FROM A MAT TO ANOTHER: Although your images can be moved around just a single mat, you can likewise move the images from a mat to another without having to go back to the Design canvas to change colors. This can be done by clicking the three tiny dots positioned at the uppermost left side corner of that image you're currently working on. Once you've done that, select the Move to Another Mat option. Then you will be allowed to choose the mat you want that image to be on. You'll easily notice the change.

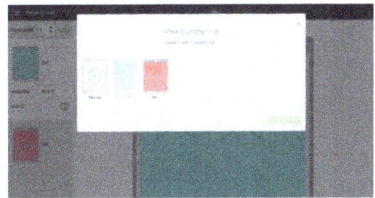

This feature can be used anytime to conserve materials. If you're skillful enough, you can arrange all your images to fit into a single mat. This is also a perfect way of quickly changing the colors on designs without having to exit the Cut screen to manually modify the color of the designs.

RE-CUT OR SKIP MATS: This feature will prove useful to you if you just know how to use it on the Cut screen. After sending your designs for cutting, the remaining processes don't require much attention. As long as your Cricut machine is fed with the correct paper color and size just exactly as the Cut screen illustrates it, you shouldn't worry about the results; your project should come out precisely the way you designed it. Nonetheless, you may find yourself wanting to re-cut a particular mat after cutting it the first time or wishing to skip the mat that is next in line. The good news is that can be done easily without you needing to exit the Cut screen.

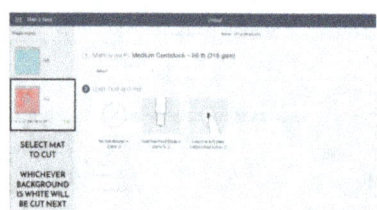

However, you need to do this before you load your

mat into the machine. You're free to select a particular mat you wish to cut manually by merely clicking or selecting the mat by the left-hand side of the Cut screen. The mat you handpicked will be skipped automatically by the cutting machine.

Moreover, if there is a particular mat you would like to re-cut, even after there're cut-marks all over it showing that the mat has been worked on already, return to the Cut screen and select that particular mat you want to manually re-cut. The Cricut machine will handle the rest automatically. However, much care must be taken when you re-cut or skip mats. Ensure you always double-check if what you're loading into the machine fits perfectly into the emphasized mat on the Cut Screen. A lot of Cricut users make mistakes so many times whenever they re-cut or skip mats without full attention.

SAVING COMMONLY-USED MATERIALS: Many Cricut users always feel stunned when they learn about this particular feature after using the Cricut software for a long time. They realized how much they'd missed! You're certainly missing so much if you're not making use of the Custom materials option. A lot of people, especially those people making use of the Explore Air 2 series, do not make use of this feature unintentionally because their Cricut machine is set to Vinyl, Iron-in, Cardstock, etc. Only people that use the Cricut Maker machine can notice the "Custom materials" function within the Design Space easily since there is no available option to choose the material you are cutting.

You don't have to go through the stress of strolling through more than a hundred custom materials to find the common Cardstock, Vinyl and Iron-on Vinyl settings over and over again. You can just add each one of these to the Favorite box. It shouldn't take you more than a few minutes to stroll through the Materials menu and locate the materials that you make use of regularly. Just click on the star positioned under the Materials menu and then proceed to select "Favorites" instead of "Popular" on that same menu. Once you've done that, all that will be left is just a menu showing all the materials you mostly cut. That is way easier and comfortable, right?

CONNECTING TWO OR MORE CRICUT MACHINES SIMULTANEOUSLY: Even though a typical Cricut user doesn't often make use of more than a single Cricut machine, it's possible to connect more than one machine to your Design Space account at the same time. You can do this by either using Bluetooth when using a wireless machine model or using USB with your PC. Moreover, you shouldn't worry about getting your machines and your designs mixed up during the cutting session. The number of Cricut machines you connect to your Design Space doesn't matter. The first step you'll take when you reach the Cut screen is to select which machine you want to use to cut your design. You will find this function in a drop-down menu located at the top. With this step, Cricut ensures that its users can stay assured that they're using the intended machine for their project all the time.

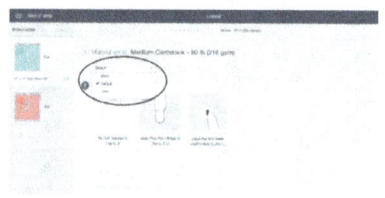

MIRROR SETTING: There're times when Cricut users have to do their design cutting in reverse, particularly when they are working with projects with Iron-on. This process of reversing is known as "Mirror." Although your designs can always be flipped on your Canvas screen horizontally, there is also an option provided to mirror designs while using the Cut screen.

This setting doesn't only enable you to mirror the images or mats you want to flip; it also allows you to create and adjust your designs without having to flip them on the Canvas screen. It gets easier to view and customize your designs on the mat.

FILLING YOUR MAT BY ADJUSTING PROJECT COPIES: A lot of Cricut users don't get to use this cool Auto-fill function, either by unawareness or unavailability. This function can only be accessed on Cricut machine models that are old. Using the old machine models, a single star can be put on your Canvas, and you can select your paper size manually and then select "Auto-fill" without stress. Once you click on "Auto-fill," your Cricut machine will fill up the paper with stars automatically, fitting in as many stars as your paper can comfortably take. Even though you will not find this function in the most recent Design Space, there is an easy way of doing almost the same thing this function does.

A LITTLE BIT MORE...

Learning to use the "Cricut" machine involves a steep learning curve. The most complicated aspect of this is using the "Design Space" software to hone various features and tools to help you create your designs and turn your "inspiration into creation." There are multiple shortcuts on the "Design Space" app to make your design not only easy but more efficient. We'll cover them in 3 different sections, starting with the "Design Space" app, the device, tools, and accessories "Cricut," as well as select the cutting material and conclude with how you can clean the machine to make it work like new.

Design Space application

1. The "Section" tool can be used to cut a design from an image by cropping or use your search keywords wisely. The search functionality within the "Design Space" is not very dynamic, so your choice of keywords will make a big difference in the designs and projects displayed to you. For example, if you search for images containing dotted designs and search with the keyword "Dots," you will be provided with about 140 images, but if you search with the term "Dot," I would see almost twice as many images. You should also search with synonyms and closely related terms of your target design idea. For instance, if you would like to create a Halloween project, you can search with terms like pumpkin, costumes, and tricks or treat, among others You can look at every the pictures related to your project.

1. The "Cartridge" image sets. It is likely that during your research, you like a design more than anything else made available to you, but it's not exactly how you want it to look. Well, just click on the small information circle(s) at

the bottom of the image, and you'll be able to view the entire set of images or "cartridge" of images similar to the selected image within the "Design Space Image Library."

1. Use the "Hide" tool to cut images from the canvas selectively. When you're trying to turn your imagination into a work of art, you may want to see and draw inspiration from multiple images as you work on your design. But once you have your desired design, you don't want to cut every other image on the canvas. This is where the "Hide" tool comes in handy, so you don't need to delete images on the canvas to avoid cutting them along with your design. To hide the image, you just need to click on the "eye" symbol next to those specific image layers on the "Layers Panel." The hidden images will not be deleted from the canvas, but they will not appear on the cutting mat when you click the "Render" button to cut the design.

1. A treasure trove of free fonts and images. As a beginner, you want to use many free fonts and images to get your hands-on experience with your "Cricut" device. It is an excellent way of spending less money and still be able to create beautiful craft projects. Within the "Design Space" app, you can click the "Filter" icon next to the search bar (available within the images, fonts, and projects tabs) and select "Free" to view only the free resources within each category.

1. Use synchronized colors to save time and money. This is a great tool when you have designs that are a composite of multiple images or inherently contain different shades of the same color. Instead of using five different shades of the same color, you can synchronize the colors to only use one color sheet. You just need to click on "Color Synchronization" tab on the "Layers Panel" in the upper right corner of the screen. Then drag the desired layers of your project to the target color layer, and the moved layer will immediately be changed to have the same

color as the target color. removing it, as shown in the following image.

1. You can use the "Section" tool to crop the image. The "Design Space" application still lacks the "Crop" feature, so if you need to crop an image, you will need to be creative. A good tip is to use the "Section" tool and the "Shapes" to get the image you want.

1. Ability to edit design lines to cut, mark or draw. With the latest version of the "Design Space" application, you can simply change the "Linetype" of a design from the default type to the desired action instead of searching for designs with a default line type that meets the needs of your design. For example, if the selected project is set to "Linetype" Cut but you want the project to be "Linetype," you can easily change the "Linetype" by clicking on the "Linetype" drop-down list and making your selection.

1. Power of the "Pattern" tool. As you learned from the last project in this book, "Custom Refrigerator Magnets," you can use your uploaded images to be used as pattern fillers for your designs. You'll also be able to edit the image template and patterns that already exist within the "Design Space" application to create your own unique and custom patterns. The "Edit Pattern" window lets you adjust the resolution and placement of the pattern on your design and much more. To use the "Pattern" feature, you must use the "Print and Cut" approach for your project, with access to a printer.

1. Change the position of your design on the cutting mat. When you're ready to cut your design and click the "Make It" button, you'll notice that your design will be aligned in the upper left corner of the mat. Now, if you are using material previously cut in the upper left corner, simply drag and move the image on the "Design Space" mat to meet the placement

of the cutting material. You will cut the image anywhere on the mat by moving the design to that specific location on the mat.

1. Use the standard "keyboard shortcuts." The "Design Space" application has all the necessary tools and buttons (refer to Chapter 2 for a list of all buttons and their uses) to allow you to edit images and fonts. Still, if you prefer to use keyboard shortcuts to edit the image quickly, the "Design Space" application will support this. The following keyboard shortcuts are available: "Copy (Ctrl + C)"; "Paste (Ctrl + V)"; "Delete (Delete key)"; "Copy (Ctrl + Z)".

1. Moving the design from one mat to another. Yes! Not only can you move the design on the mat itself, but you can also move the design from one mat to another simply by clicking on the three dots (...) above the mat and selecting "Move to another mat." A popup window will then appear to select from the

existing mats for the design to use as a new mat for the selected design.

1. Choose to repeat cutting the same mat or skip a mat from the cut altogether. By following the instructions on the "Design Space" and feeding the right color and size of the material to the machine, you will be able to cut your design perfectly. You can change the order in which the mats are cut, repeat the cutting of the desired mat, and even skip cutting a mat if necessary. You can do this easily by simply clicking and selecting the mat you would like to cut.

1. Save the cut materials as Favorites for quick access. Instead of spending time filtering and searching for cut material on the "Design Space" app repeatedly, just save frequently used material by clicking the star next to the "Cricut" logo on the "Design Space" app to save them in the "Favorites" tab next to the default "All Materials" tab. When you're

getting ready to cut your project, under the "Set Material" tab, the "Favorites" material will be displayed on the screen.

1. The "Weld," "Contour," and "Slice" feature to customize your designs. These three tools will be activated at the bottom of the screen for projects that allow these changes. The "Weld" tool will allow you to combine two different projects to get a composite design, with no remaining seams and cut lines that might be present on the individual projects. This helps you get a single continuous cut for your plan, so you don't have to glue and assemble multiple pieces to get the final design, such as creating cake toppers, gift tags, and other decorations. The "Outline" tool can be used to turn on or off any cut line in any cut file and thus allow you to customize the image in various ways. So imagine you have a picture of a flower and you want to remove design details and get more than one outline of the flower; you can do this by clicking the "Contour" button in the lower part of the screen and selecting the

different elements of the image you want to turn on or off from the outline pop-up window.

1. You can store your most frequently used cut materials on "Cricut Maker." Unlike the "Cricut Explore" series, which has call settings for a variety of commonly used cut materials, the "Cricut Maker" requires you to use a "Custom Materials" menu within the "Design Space" application, which you can access using the button on the machine with the "Cricut" logo, as there is no dial available to choose the material you want to cut.

1. "Cricut Access Membership" - With a monthly fee of about $10 or an annual membership fee, you will be able to use a wider variety of free fonts and images. You'll be able to freely use 50K+ images, 400+ fonts, and thousands of designs, saving a great deal of money in the long term, depending on your use.

1. You can change the cutting settings of the materials. Even after selecting the default settings to cut the desired material, you may notice that the material may not be cut as desired. To help with this, "Design Space" allows you to adjust the cutting settings for all materials, such as the depth of cut, the cutting blade, and the number of passes that the "Cricut" device should make. Since this might not be so intuitive for most beginners, here is a detailed walkthrough of this process: when using the "Cricut Maker," select "Materials" on the cutting screen and, if using the "Cricut Explore" series, set the dial to "Custom."

Click on "Browse all materials" at the top of the menu.

At the bottom of the screen, select "Material Settings."

The pop-up window for "Custom Materials" will be displayed in the following image, where you can make the required adjustments.

1. Adjust the pressure at which the material can

be cut. You may want to simply adjust the pressure at which the cutting is done to achieve a clean and neat cut of the fabric without having to go through the process above to adjust the cutting setting of the material. Once you have selected your cutting material, you will see a drop-down option with the "Default" setting on the cutting screen. Simply click on the drop-down button and adjust the pressure to "More" or "Less."

CHAPTER FIVE

PROJECTS FOR BEGINNERS

PAPER BOUQUET

MATERIALS:

- Cardstock
- Glue gun
- LightGrip cutting mat
- Weeding tool or pick
- Green pipe cleaners or floral wire

Directions:

1. Open Cricut Design Space and create a new

project.
2. Select the "Image" button in the lower left-hand corner and search for "paper flowers."
3. Select the image with several flower pieces and click "Insert."
4. Copy the flowers and resize them for variety in your bouquet.
5. Place your cardstock on the cutting mat.
6. Send the design to your Cricut.
7. Remove the outer edge of the paper, leaving the flowers on the mat.
8. Use your weeding tool or carefully pick to remove the flowers from the mat.
9. Glue the flower pieces together in the centers, with the largest petals at the bottom.
10. Bend or curl petals as desired to create multiple looks.
11. Glue the flowers to the ends of the pipe cleaners or sections of floral wire.
12. Gather your flowers together in a vase or wrap them with tissue paper.
13. Enjoy your beautiful bouquet!

LEAFY GARLAND

Materials:

- Cardstock—2 or more colors of green or white to paint yourself Glue gun
- LightGrip cutting mat
- Weeding tool or pick
- Floral wire
- Floral tape

Directions:

1. Open Cricut Design Space and create a new project.
2. Select the "Image" button in the lower left-hand corner and search for "leaf collage."
3. Select the image of leaves and click "Insert."
4. Place your cardstock on the cutting mat.
5. Send the design to your Cricut.
6. Remove the outer edge of the paper, leaving the leaves on the mat.
7. Use a pick or scoring tool to score down the center of each leaf lightly.
8. Use your weeding tool or carefully pick to remove the leaves from the mat.
9. Gently bend each leaf at the scoreline.
10. Glue the leaves into bunches of two or three.
11. Cut a length of floral wire to your desired garland size and wrap the ends with floral tape.

12. Attach the leaf bunches to the wire using floral tape.
13. Continue attaching leaves until you have a garland of the size you want. Bundle lots of leaves for a really full look, or spread them out to be sparser.
14. Create hooks at the ends of the garland with floral wire.
15. Hang your beautiful leaf garland wherever you'd like!

EASY ENVELOPE ADDRESSING

Materials:

- Envelopes to address
- Cricut Pen Tool
- LightGrip cutting mat

Directions:

1. Open Cricut Design Space and create a new project.
2. Create a box the appropriate size for your envelopes.
3. Select the "Text" button in the lower left-hand corner.

4. Choose one handwriting font for a uniform look or different fonts for each line to mix it up.
5. Type your return address in the upper left-hand corner of the design.
6. Type the "to" address in the center of the design.
7. Insert your Cricut pen into the auxiliary holder of your Cricut, making sure it is secure.
8. Place your cardstock on the cutting mat.
9. Send the design to your Cricut.
10. Remove your envelope and repeat as needed.
11. Send out your "hand-lettered" envelopes!

WATERCOLOR HEART SIGN

Materials:

- Watercolor paper
- Watercolor paints and paintbrush
- Glue
- LightGrip cutting mat
- Weeding tool or pick
- Frame

Directions:

1. Paint your watercolor paper in soft gradients. Use a lot of water and gradually blend two or three colors into each other. Set aside to dry.
2. Open Cricut Design Space and create a new project.
3. Select the "Image" button in the lower left-hand corner and search for "heart."
4. Select the heart of your choice and click "Insert."
5. Place your watercolor paper on the cutting mat.
6. Send the design to your Cricut.
7. Remove the outer edge of the paper, leaving the heart on the mat.
8. Use your weeding tool or carefully pick to remove the heart from the mat.
9. Glue your heart to the center of a blank piece of paper, cut to fit your frame.
10. Place your sign into your frame.
11. Set or hang wherever you need a little color!

PATTERNED GIFT WRAP

Materials:

- White kraft paper
- Cricut Pen Tool in color(s) of your choice

- 12x24 cutting mat
- Weeding tool or pick

Directions:

1. Open Cricut Design Space and create a new project.
2. Select the "Image" button in the lower left-hand corner and search for doodled images appropriate for the gift you're wrapping, for example, "Christmas doodle" or "birthday doodle."
3. Select the images you like and click "Insert."
4. Copy, resize and rotate the images to create a pattern you like for the size of your wrapping paper.
5. Change the colors of the doodles if desired—leaving them black creates a coloring-book feel, or you can make them in different colors.
6. Place your paper on the cutting mat.
7. Send the design to your Cricut.
8. Remove your wrapping paper from the mat.
9. Wrap your gift in your customized wrapping paper!

BIRTHDAY STAR CUPCAKE TOPPERS

Materials:

- Cardstock—Glittery gold and white
- Glue stick
- Glue gun
- LightGrip cutting mat
- Weeding tool or pick
- Toothpicks

Directions:

1. Open Cricut Design Space and create a new project.
2. Select the "Image" button in the lower left-hand corner and search for "star."
3. Select the star you like best and click "Insert."
4. Place your gold cardstock on the cutting mat.
5. Send the design to your Cricut.
6. In Design Space, select the "Text" button in the lower left-hand corner.
7. Choose your favorite font and type "Happy birthday!"
8. Place your white cardstock on the cutting mat.
9. Send the design to your Cricut.

10. Remove the outer edge of the paper, leaving the text on the mat.
11. Use your weeding tool or carefully pick to remove the text from the mat.
12. Use the glue stick to attach the text on top of the stars.
13. Use the glue gun to attach toothpicks to the back of each star.
14. Stick your toppers onto your cupcakes!

HOLIDAY GIFT CARD HOLDERS

Materials:

- Holiday-themed scrapbook paper
- Cricut Scoring Stylus
- LightGrip cutting mat
- Weeding tool or pick
- Glue stick
- Ribbon, twine, or string to match your paper

Directions:

1. Open Cricut Design Space and create a new project.
2. Select the "Image" button in the lower left-hand corner and search for "gift card."

3. Select the gift cardholder template and click "Insert."
4. Insert the scoring stylus into the Cricut making sure it is secure.
5. Place your paper on the cutting mat.
6. Send the design to your Cricut.
7. Use the weeding tool or carefully pick to remove the template from the mat.
8. Bend the large outer piece and the inner cardholder where they have been scored.
9. Bend the three tabs on the inner cardholder inward and the one tab on the other side outward.
10. Apply glue to the three tabs and attach them.
11. Glue the inner cardholder to the large outer piece with the outward-facing tab.
12. Glue two decorative pieces to the inside and two to the outside.
13. Place the gift card in the holder and tie it closed with ribbon, twine, or string.
14. Present your gift card to the receiver!

THANK YOU CARD

Materials:

- Cardboard

- Cricut Pen—this will enable you to write professionally on the card.

Directions:

1. Again you'll need to access Design Space to find the perfect design for your thank-you card. There are hundreds to choose from or you can create your own image and message.
2. Send your design to the Cricut machine and make sure your cardboard is in the machine. Your machine will cut it effortlessly for you.
3. There is a feature in Design Space that allows you to write and cut. If you activate this, you'll be able to write your message directly onto the card and the machine will cut as you go. This allows you to add it to the card you are creating and make it look 3D.
4. The machine does the cutting for you so you don't need to worry if you are pressing hard enough.
5. Your design may need a secondary layer to create the right effect. The machine will tell you when to change the material.
6. All you need to do is slide the two pieces together at the end.

COLORING PAGES

Materials:

- Paper or a card
- Cricut Pen—as explained above
- StandardGrip cutting mat

Directions:

1. Go into the Design Space app and select the "insert shapes" option. You'll need to insert a shape that is the same size as your finished coloring page. You can always start small and create a bigger one on your second attempt.
2. Now click on the "insert images" button and find anything that you would like to make a coloring sheet.
3. You'll need to click on it to select it and add it to your design.
4. You can add more than one image if you wish.
5. Now click the image and select the "ungroup" option. You can then select each element and

change it from scissors to pen. This means it will not be cut out.
6. You'll then need to regroup all the pieces.
7. Once you're happy with the finished look, you can send it to your Cricut machine. It will print it and cut the outline at the same time.

GIFT TAGS

Materials:

- Card
- Selection of Cricut pens
- StandardGrip mat

Directions:

1. The first thing is to enter the Design Space app and choose the image or images you wish to display on your gift tag.
2. As part of this, you'll need to decide what colors each part of your image should be.
3. Send the image to your Cricut machine. Don't forget to add a small hole where the ribbon will go through.
4. A nice touch is to print letters or an image

separately. Design Space can help you to create these and add tabs that will help you to either stick them to the gift tag or hook them into it.
5. Now, all you need to do is join the pieces together. You can use your weeding tool to tidy up any difficult areas.
6. The draw layers can drastically improve the look of your gift tag. You can also add glitter to the finished article to add an extra effect.

ST. PATRICK'S DAY SHIRT

Materials:

- Machine to cut Cricut maker
- Cricut Space Development account
- Cut design with shamrock and doodles
- Infusible Pen Ink 0.04-Green
- Cricut Space Access Design
- Infusible Cricut Tin Jacket
- Easy Press 2 Print
- Card Warehouse
- Butcher Text
- Paper on Laser Printer

Directions:

1. Activate, and size, the Design Space Cut File to fit your shirt.
2. Send out to cut (draw) the project. Don't forget to have an image mirror. Place the paper with Laser Printer on a StandardGrip cutting mat. Make sure to follow the Infusible Ink Pen prompts.
3. Delete the laser printer paper from the cutting mat once the image has been drawn.
4. Place a cardstock sheet inside the shirt where you want your design to be.
5. Place on the shirt, image side down, the laser printer paper with design.
6. Load the butcher paper to the laser printer.
7. Following Cricut's recommended heat setting, press the image onto the shirt with the Easy Press.
8. Remove from the shirt the butcher paper, laser printer paper and card stock and be St. Paddy's Day pinch-proof.
9. If you're acquainted with the cutting Cricut machine family, you're familiar with all of the various projects done by you with these instruments, too. The electronic cutting machine or Cricut Joy appears to fit in right with a large variety of material that the cutting tool can cut.

TRICK OR TREAT BAGS

Materials:

- Packs of the medium canvas (primary or neon)
- Vinyl iron-on with the perfect colors
- Cricut Discover or another computer for vinyl cutting
- If you own a Cricut and you choose to use the same version, the Cricut Design Space File
- Using iron
- Cloth Pressing

Directions:

1. Cut out the patterns on the cutting machine that you have selected. You can press the link above to get the interface I used for my bags if you are using a Cricut. My build was around 4'x6', which was a decent size to fit in front of the bag, and there was always plenty of space on the edges. When you cut the pattern, make sure to mirror the image for iron-on.
2. Your template is put on the bag wherever you

want it to be once you have cut and weeded it. You might want to iron the bag a little bit first because some of my bags were a little wrinkled. In compliance with the guidelines for the sort of vinyl you are using, put your printing cloth over the surface and iron it on. Peel the backup and you're out. Amazingly fast.
3. It only took me a couple of minutes to make all six bags for my kids and I think they turn out to be very cool. Great for a busy period around Halloween. To see all the items they have for Halloween and other upcoming holidays, be able to reach over to the Oriental Trading Firm.

DESIGNING SPIDER WEBS

Materials:

- Gun Quick Glue
- Cricut Maker
- Rotary Blade
- Cricut Design
- Mat Cloth

Directions:

HOME MADE CRAFTING   87

1. I began by making a felt table runner with a spider. With the Cricut Creator and rotary cutter, you can use any sort of felt, but I have considered the Cricut felt sheet to become the best for not having lint behind with the mat.
2. At Cricut Design Room, I built a template for two separate wide spider nets.
3. Open the file Template Space and press the Make It button in grey. Select two project copies when you get to the mat overview, then press Request. Choose Begin.
4. Select 2 Copies of the Project.
5. From the cutting machine, pick your Cricut Maker. From the materials collection, pick Felt. Click Edit Software to encourage you to click a Rotary Blade.
6. Use the Cricut Maker to pick a rotary blade to cut felt.
7. Use the Cricut Tool to cut out all the felt. You will have big and small spider webs, two black spider webs and two little red circles when you are done.
8. Split the felt utilizing the Cricut Maker.
9. The felt spider web pulls very quickly right off the mat, but on it, you are left with a lot of little felt bits. You should use an XL scraper

to easily clean your mat. For cardstock, this fits well, too.
10. Using the XL scraper to wipe up material scraps.
11. Using hot glue to tie the red circles, cut out on the giant spider net fragments behind the hourglass.
12. To connect the red felt patch, use hot glue to tie the black spider webs in lines, alternating colors, to the white spider webs. I'm so impressed at how easily the Maker can carve so cleanly and precisely those complicated cuts.

A TABLE LAMP

Materials:

- A lamp; you're not making the actually electric part!
- Adhesive vinyl
- Transfer Tape

Directions:

1. Go into Design Space and select a design that you like. Don't forget that it needs to let some light through; a completely black light shade will not give a great effect!
2. You need to select a piece of vinyl that fits your lampshade. This will give you the dimensions you need when creating your image.
3. Slide your vinyl into the Cricut machine and then send the image to be cut. This may take a few minutes depending on the intricacy of your design!
4. You can now remove the vinyl and carefully weed the fabric to ensure the design is completely removed from the backing piece.
5. Take your time with this; ideally, you don't want to do it a second time!
6. Carefully clean the surface of your lamp. It needs to be free of dust, grease and to be fully dry before you can add your vinyl.
7. Apply the transfer tape to your vinyl image. Carefully remove the backing and use the transfer tape to hold the image together as you move it across to your lampshade.
8. This will need to be mirrored if you have added words into your design. If you don't, the words will be backward!

9. Rub the adhesive vinyl gently to ensure it is fully stuck to your lampshade. You can then remove the transfer tape and enjoy the finished lamp.

Note: Don't directly stick it directly on your lightbulb. It will burn!

XMAS DECORATION

Materials

- Card
- Adhesive vinyl
- Adhesive foil
- Cricut pens

Directions:

1. Locate your desired image in Design Space or draw/write your own using the Cricut pen.
2. It is a good idea to use a layered effect to create a more interesting decoration. You can even opt to use different materials for each layer. The app will guide you through the necessary steps.
3. For example, you can write a message in

black on white card and have the machine cut it out. This can then be adhered to a red card cut into a shape by your machine.
4. Add some images and writing on foil to improve the overall effect of your decoration and then adhere them to a piece of vinyl. Make sure the image is evenly placed.
5. The vinyl can be hung to create an enticing effect. However, you can also purchase clear plastic baubles and stick the adhesive vinyl to them. You'll need to use transfer tape to achieve the right result.
6. This is one project that improves with experimentation!

WALL ART

Materials:

- A wood frame or some wood to make your own
- Stapler
- Canvas

Directions:

1. Measure the size of your frame and add one

inch to the measurements. This is the size of the canvas you need. If you're making your own frame, then you can select the size of your image.
2. Go into Design Space and choose an image you like. You'll need to create a blank space first the same size as the inside of your frame, not your canvas piece.
3. You can then insert your image into this space.
4. As before, you'll need to ungroup the image and change each element from scissors to pen. Unless your image is supposed to have sections cut out in which case leave them like scissors.
5. This can actually be a good way of creating layers and altering the final appeal of your art.
6. Now, print your work of art onto the canvas, using your Cricut machine to get the lines right.
7. This canvas can then be wrapped around your frame and stapled to the inside of your frame to hold it tight.
8. If you're making your own frame, you can adhere the canvas to the wood and glue the

wood together to create the same level of tightness.
9. Now, hang your work of art and admire it!

WATERCOLOR HEART SIGN

Supplies Needed:

- Watercolor paper
- Watercolor paints and paintbrush
- Glue
- LightGrip cutting mat
- Weeding tool or pick
- Frame

Directions:

1. Paint your watercolor paper in soft gradients. Use a lot of water and gradually blend two or three colors into each other. Set it aside to dry.
2. Open Cricut Design Space and create a new project.
3. Select the "Image" button in the lower left-hand corner and search for "heart."
4. Select the heart of your choice and click "Insert."

5. Place your watercolor paper on the cutting mat.
6. Send the design to your Cricut.
7. Remove the outer edge of the paper, leaving the heart on the mat.
8. Use your weeding tool or carefully pick to remove the heart from the mat.
9. Glue your heart to the center of a blank piece of paper, cut to fit your frame.
10. Place your sign into your frame.
11. Set or hang wherever you need a little color!

PATTERNED GIFT WRAP

Supplies Needed:

- White kraft paper
- Cricut Pen Tool in color(s) of your choice
- 12x24 cutting mat
- Weeding tool or pick

Directions:

1. Open Cricut Design Space and create a new project.
2. Select the "Image" button in the lower left-hand corner and search for doodled images

appropriate for the gift you're wrapping, for example, "Christmas doodle" or "birthday doodle."
3. Select the images you like and click "Insert."
4. Copy, resize and rotate the images to create a pattern you like for the size of your wrapping paper.
5. Change the colors of the doodles if desired—leaving them black creates a coloring-book feel, or you can make them in different colors.
6. Place your paper on the cutting mat.
7. Send the design to your Cricut.
8. Remove your wrapping paper from the mat.
9. Wrap your gift in your customized wrapping paper!

VINYL CHALKBOARD

Supplies Needed:

- Cricut Explore 2
- Standard Grip mat
- Cricut Linen vinyl in desired colors
- Weeder, transfer tape
- Chalkboard and chalk pen

Directions:

1. Log into the "Design Space" application and click on the "New Project" button on the top right corner of the screen to view a blank canvas.
2. Click on the "Projects" icon and type in "Vinyl Chalkboard" in the search bar.
3. Click on "Customize" to further edit the project to your preference, or simply click on the "Make It" button and load the vinyl sheet to your Cricut machine. Using a Weeder tool, remove the negative space pieces of the design.
4. Use the transfer tape to apply the vinyl cuts to the chalkboard. Then use the scraper tool on top of the transfer tape to remove any bubbles and then just peel off the transfer tape.
5. Lastly, use a chalk pen to write messages.

VINYL HERRINGBONE BRACELET

Supplies Needed:

- Cricut Maker or Cricut Explore
- Standard Grip mat

- Vinyl (midnight)
- Weeder
- Scraper
- Transfer tape
- Metal bracelet gold

Directions:

1. Log into the "Design Space" application and click on the "New Project" button on the top right corner of the screen to view a blank canvas.
2. Click on the "Images" icon on the "Design Panel" and type in "M33278" in the search bar. Select the image and click on the "Insert Images" button at the bottom of the screen.
3. Click on "Customize" to further edit the project to your preference, or simply click on the "Make It" button and load the vinyl sheet to your Cricut machine and follow the directions on the screen to cut your project.
4. Using a Weeder tool, remove the negative space pieces of the design. Use the transfer tape to apply the vinyl cuts to the bracelet. Then use the scraper tool on top of the transfer tape to remove any bubbles and then just peel off the transfer tape.

TREASURE CHEST JEWELRY BOX

Supplies Needed:

- Plain wooden box with lid
- White vinyl
- Vinyl transfer tape
- Cutting mat
- Weeding tool or pick
- Small blade

Directions:

1. Select the "Image" button in the lower left-hand corner and search for "keyhole."
2. Click your favorite keyhole design and click "Insert."
3. Select the "Text" button in the lower left-hand corner.
4. Choose your favorite font and type "Treasure."
5. Place your vinyl on the cutting mat.
6. Send the design to Cricut.
7. Make use of a weeding tool or pick to remove the excess vinyl from the design.
8. Apply separate pieces of transfer tape to the keyhole and the word.

9. Remove the paper backing from the tape on the keyhole.
10. Place the keyhole where the lid and box meet so that half is on the lid and half is on the box.
11. Rub the tape to transfer the vinyl to the wood, making sure there are no bubbles. Carefully peel the tape away.
12. Use a sharp blade to cut the keyhole design in half so that the box can open.
13. Transfer the word to the front of the box using the same method.
14. Optional: Add details with paint or markers to make the box look more like a treasure chest. Add wood grain, barnacles, seashells, or pearls.
15. Store your jewelry in your new treasure chest.

CUPCAKE WRAPPERS

Materials:

- Paper or card

Directions:

1. Take a look at the Design Space site and

select the design or designs that appeal to you the most. The great thing about these designs is that you can create more than you need and save the extra for another occasion.
2. Your image will need to be approximately 9-inches long to wrap around a standard cupcake.
3. Load your card to the machine and send the image or images. Within a few minutes, they should all be printed and cut.
4. Wrap the card around your cupcake and clip it together by making a small incision in each end. If you've used an actual cupcake design from Design Space, the tab will already be present.

An alternative is to overlap the end and use a dot of glue to hold the two ends together.

Top Tip: When doing a children's party, you can actually create the designs and get the children to decorate them before you wrap them around the cupcakes.

CHRISTMAS SWEET JARS

Materials:

- Scraper

- Tape Move
- Vinyl Glue
- Device for Weeding
- Similar Gifts
- Container of Glass
- Mat Cutting

Directions:

1. Work in Cricut Software, but in Silhouette Studio you could also do this. Download the template and change the colors to fit the vinyl shades you are going to use.
2. Select the "Make It" button and you will be directed by the program through the steps of charging and slicing each individual vinyl paint.

Note: sticky vinyl is put on the cutting mat with the colored side face up, and the plain sheet covering facing up on the sheet.

Stage Two: Prototypes for Cut and Weeding:

1. Strip the unwanted design from across the models after the slicing is complete, then weed out the smaller pieces.
2. To add firm pressure, cut the tape's top to

match over the template and use the scraper method.
3. To burnish well on the logo, line the open spaces on the container and use the scraper method again. When you operate on a curved surface, beginning from the middle and working your way back, it is simpler to implement the pattern.
4. Remove the transfer film, leaving only the vinyl decal behind.
5. To implement the second part of the template, repeat the steps above.
6. The container looks so festive and cute and couldn't have been simpler to do.

**Optional: Making Customized Items:
Fill and Supply with Presents!**

1. With some new cheesecakes, sweets, colored wrappers, cotton candy, mini gummy bears, Christmas-shaped towels and those cool design tent key rings, I filled up this nice little container.
2. With a festive bow, tie it all together and leave it on the door for a nice surprise!

FATHER'S DAY MUG

Materials:

- Stuff
- Cricut machine and Cricut Design Space
- SVG cut file produced by Jen Goode for Father's Day
- Vinyl Blue
- A cup or mug

Directions:

1. Use the Cricut system to build the SVG template of a personalized Father's Day mug —Jen Goode. This kit includes both the PNG 1 layer and the SVG 1 layer format. One of two layers is also available commercially if you want a more complex layout. Simply ungroup the file to use the double layer file once you have entered it into the Cricut Template Room. You'll then adjust the colors of the layers if you like.
2. Download and upload the file that was cut from the SVG to the Cricut Machine Space.
3. Set the file to the size you'd want and look at

it. I sized my mug to around 3.5" high. The on-screen directions for cutting the word art.

4. The leftover vinyl that falls from your building needs to be weeded.
5. Use the transfer tape, place the word art on the dry and clean side of the cup. To fit in, burnish.
6. That's it! Simple and super-fast, huh?
7. Humor from Cut Dad Jen Goode's designed word painting. Then, the transfer tape is used with vinyl word art to modify the cup. Build a gift for your dad. Word art is a great source of DIY crafts for every type of style.

MODEL AIRPLANE

Materials:

- Two pieces of 1/32-inch thick balsa wood
- Dark stain
- Ivory adhesive vinyl
- Superglue or wood glue

Directions:

1. This is a "Make it Now" project in Design Space, so open the library, search for the project and open the project in a new workspace. Using a Strong Grip cutting mat, lay your balsa wood pieces on and make sure to adjust your settings to "custom" on your machine. When you are ready, send your project to cut. If the machine does not cut through the first time, repeat cutting, without moving your mat, three or four more times.
2. Gently remove the wood pieces from your mat. This is fragile wood, so be very careful removing the pieces so you do not break them. Lay your pieces to the side for now.
3. Go back to Design Space and write out the name or message you want to appear on the side of the plane. Make sure the size is correct for the size of the plane. Add your vinyl to your StandardGrip cutting mat and tell your machine to cut the image. Follow the prompts on your computer.
4. Weed out the insides of your vinyl as necessary and remove the unnecessary exterior vinyl that is not part of your design. When it is ready, lay the design on your airplane.
5. You can offer the pieces of the plane with

directions as a gift, or you can assemble the plane yourself. If you are making it, use your super glue or wood glue to securely attach all the pieces to one another and allow them to dry fully. Place this design somewhere people can enjoy your handiwork!

WEDDING INVITATION

Materials:

- Cricut Maker
- Cutting mat
- Decorative paper
- Crepe paper
- Fabric
- Home printer

Directions:

1. Log into the "Design Space" application and click on the "New Project" button on the top right corner of the screen to view a blank canvas.
2. Let's customize an already existing project by clicking on the "Projects" icon on the "Design Panel" and selecting "Cards" from the "All

Categories" drop-down, then type in "wedding invite" in the search bar.

3. For example, you could select the project shown in the picture below and click "Customize" at the bottom of the screen to edit and personalize the text of your invite.
4. Click "Text" on the "Designs Panel" and type in the details of the invite. You can change the font, color and alignment of the text from the "Edit Text Bar" on top of the screen and remember to change the "Fill" to "Print" on the top of the screen.
5. Select all the elements of the design and click on the "Group" icon on the top right of the screen under "Layers panel." Then, click on "Save" to save your project.

CONCLUSIONS

You've just become a professional Cricut user! However, it would help if you did not forget the most important things discussed in this book. If you forget things quickly, have this book with you every time you want to work on your Cricut machine.

If you have worked your way through the projects in this book, you are well on your way to becoming a Cricut pro. Like a recipe book, the projects, along with the ideas in this book, can be adjusted, adapted and added to, so that you can make each one uniquely yours.

With the Cricut, you are going to find birthdays, special occasions, seasonal holidays and even school projects to be a lot easier, as well as more personalized.

Everyone loves receiving gifts, cards and so on, that have been designed especially for them.

Since the development of the Amazon platform, more and more people have started to develop their products using Cricut technology. We've all been told to look for products on the Chinese markets, buy massive quantities and get the products at meager prices. Some people prefer to use the Cricut machine to create their decorations, while others can even make some money out of their projects. Just think of customized T-shirts or mugs, as these items are trendy today.

Owning this type of machine is a great opportunity for many people to expand their crafting abilities and it's great if you want to branch out and explore new things as a crafter as well because you can add so many new things to their repertoire. This machine can literally have endless possibilities for a crafter as a result. You can make or you can print on just about anything. For example, if you are a vinyl lover, you could have an endless supply of things that you can put vinyl on such as glasses, mugs and a plethora of other options.

www.ingramcontent.com/pod-product-compliance
Lightning Source LLC
Chambersburg PA
CBHW070926080526
44589CB00013B/1440